Finding Birds in Mor

Introduction

On 15th April 2009, I was birding at Oukaimeden in Dominic Mitchell and a group of friends who had jus the desert areas. Since I'd just been to the places the ....ng ιοr, I was able to give them up-to-date directions and sketch maps for exactly where to find species such as Scrub Warbler, Egyptian Nightjar, Saharan Olivaceous Warbler, Desert Sparrow, Dupont's Lark, Mourning Wheatear and Crowned Sandgrouse. Dominic later got in touch to say that my advice had been spot-on and that they'd managed to find all the species they'd wanted to see. The aim of this book is to give you that very same advantage for your next trip to Morocco.

To some extent, it is an update of my previous book, Finding Birds in Southern Morocco. I have chosen to change the title because many birders might regard 'southern morocco' as including the 'Western Sahara' areas as far as Dakhla. This book doesn't go THAT far south – it concentrates on the various types of desert areas between Goulimine and Merzouga and also includes 'desert' habitats in the Sous valley and, further north, near Zeida. The rest of Morocco, at least from the Oued Massa northwards, is covered in my other book, 'Finding Birds in Morocco: coasts and mountains'.

To give you an even better idea of many of the sites described in this book, I have produced an accompanying DVD of the same title. Not only do the images of the landscapes help you to locate the exact roosting holes for the Pharaoh Eagle Owl or the exact bushes for the Scrub Warblers, they also allow you to listen to the sounds of species such as Dupont's Lark, Crowned Sandgrouse, Egyptian Nightjar and both Olivaceous Warblers so you can learn how to locate them by ear. And, of course, it also provides great footage of many of Morocco's best birds, filmed using a high-definition camera.

Of course, birds move around and birding sites change so there will come a time when at least some of these birds will be best looked for elsewhere. If you visit Morocco and find you have news that would update this book, please visit www.findingbirds.com where there are site pages which cover the places in this book. Each page includes a 'comments' facility where you can add whatever you think might be useful to other readers. Some of the sites in this book are already covered by a 'birders' logbook' in a nearby café but this online feature offers the possibility of a birders logbook for every site. It should become a great asset if enough people choose to make contributions.
Have a great time in Morocco,

Dave Gosney, September 2009.

Acknowledgements

Despite making many previous trips to Morocco, I still found lots of information that was new to me by scouring a number of trip reports (eg via www.fatbirder.com), the latest edition of the book by Patrick and Fedora Bergier and the many contributions to the 'logbooks' in various Moroccan cafes. I've also appreciated the advice from birders I've met in Morocco such as Roger Sanmarti and J B Crouzier and others who have corresponded directly with me such as Steve Lister, Jon Hornbuckle, John Armitage, Richard Bonser, Sue Bryan Jos Stratford and Roger Smith . I've tried to acknowledge individual contributions within each site description – I'm sorry if I've missed anyone out. But the most special thanks must go to my wife Liz for not only putting up with my birdy cravings but even joining in with the travelling, filming, editing and designing without which none of this would be possible.

Zeida (= Zaida) plains

Attraction

A few kilometres south of Zeida is an area of plains which have become famous as the place in Morocco for Dupont's Lark. This species however is notoriously elusive. Other birds here include Red-rumped Wheatear, Desert Wheatear, Trumpeter Finch, Shore Lark, Black-bellied Sandgrouse and, sometimes, Thick-billed Lark.

Getting there

The town of Zeida is situated on route P21 between Azrou and Midelt, just south of the Middle Atlas mountains. The area for Dupont's Lark is about 3 km south of Zeida. Look for the 'crossroads' where a track crosses the main road between the two bends – it's close to the km post that says 'Er Rachidia 167' and 'Meknes 162'.

Notes

My previous book 'Finding Birds in Northern Morocco' describes the many (20+) hours I spent in the 1990's searching fruitlessly here for Dupont's Larks. I know better than most just how frustratingly elusive these birds can be. However, on my two most recent visits (in 2005 and 2009) I not only found the larks with relative ease, I also managed to film them at close quarters. I hope these notes will help you to be similarly successful. Please report your outcomes, successful or otherwise, either in the birding log at Timnay Camping or on the Zeida page at www.findingbirds.com (or both) so that others can continue to find these birds. Timing could be crucial; the larks may disappear from this area during the winter which could explain why I'd been so unsuccessful in December, February and March.

1. In mid April 2005 I was trying to get sound recordings with no traffic noise so I spent dawn at this site some distance from the road. I did hear one singing male but it had stopped singing by 06.15 after which time I failed to locate any by cold-searching.

2. I then revisited a site only 600 metres from the road (32.7944 N 4.9335 W) where I'd heard two more birds the night before. Surprisingly, although it was now over 2 hours after dawn, one of them was singing right by the track and sometimes actually sitting on top of a bush close enough for me to see its downcurved bill with the naked eye. I was able to film this bird singing and feeding (see footage in BWPi). I passed on details of it to two other crews who also saw it, in daylight at close range. In 2009 two singing birds were again audible from here but I failed to locate them on the ground.

3. Just 200 metres further on from this spot is a fork in the track (32.7948 N 4.9315 W). In 2009, after Dupont's Larks had stopped singing, I was using the vehicle as a hide to film Lesser Short-toed Larks here when a Dupont's Lark just happened to appear, feeding right beside the track. Other birds to look for on this plain include Desert Wheatear, Red-rumped Wheatear, Black-bellied Sandgrouse and Tawny Pipit. I did once have a flock of 14 Thick-billed Larks too.

4. In 2009 I also checked out a spot nearby where a contributor to the local log had easily located several singing birds. You get there by turning east from the 'z-bend' sign and following the track towards a farm for 600 metres to where it forks. Park here (32.7888 N 4.9297 W) and explore. I had three singing males at dusk and dawn including one that I managed to film beside a smaller track to the north.

5. It may be worth following the track on the opposite side of the main road, as far as the small quarry. This area has been good for Dupont's Larks in the past and I've had Trumpeter Finch, Black Wheatear, Thekla Lark, Red-rumped and Desert Wheatears, Black-bellied Sandgrouse and (possibly winter only) Short-toed and Shore Larks. One observer has reported a flock of Brown-necked Ravens here but those I've looked at carefully have definitely been Common Ravens.

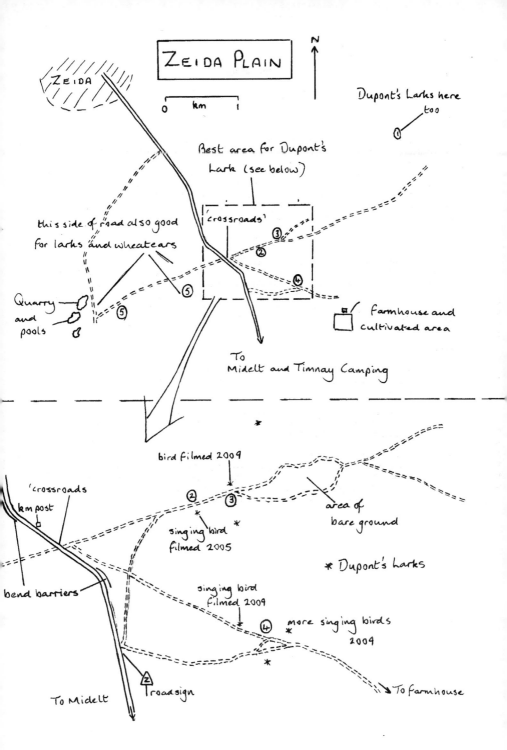

The Tafilalt

Erfoud – Merzouga - Rissani

Attraction

This is 'real desert' country. The Erg Chebbi, near Merzouga, is the most spectacular sand-dune system in Morocco. It is the best-known site in the country for Desert Sparrow. Other special birds in this area include Egyptian Nightjar, Desert Warbler, Brown-necked Raven, Fulvous Babbler, Blue-cheeked Bee-eater, Pharaoh Eagle Owl, Saharan Olivaceous Warbler, Spotted Sandgrouse and, in winter, Tristram's Warbler. Needless to say, this is the best area for 'true' desert species such as Bar-tailed Desert and Hoopoe Larks. In some years, shallow lakes form, providing the spectacle of waterbirds in the desert including flamingoes and Ruddy Shelduck. It is possible to arrange 4x4 excursions into the desert to look for Houbara Bustards.

Getting there

Erfoud is located in the Ziz valley about 75 km south of Er Rachidia. If you continue through Erfoud for a further 18 km you reach Rissani from where there is now a new tarmac road, out of the east side of town, which reaches Merzouga after a further 36 km. To reach many of the best sites, you need to go 'off piste'. In the past I've driven in ordinary cars, and even a minibus, along tracks all the way from Erfoud to Merzouga via the Auberge Derkaoua but since the opening of the new road these old tracks are no longer well-maintained so it's safer to get to the various auberges via the Rissani-Merzouga road, as described on page 10.

Notes

1. The road into the desert from Erfoud takes you as far as the Kasbah Said without difficulty. Birds to be looked for in this area include Desert Warbler, Egyptian Nightjar and Desert Sparrow (see page 6).

2. The Rissani area includes probably the best stake-outs for Pharaoh Eagle Owl, Saharan Olivaceous Warbler and Egyptian Nightjar. The oasis around the town also has birds such as Fulvous Babbler and Rufous Bush Chat (see page 8).

3. The Merzouga area includes the spectacular sand-dunes of the Erg Chebbi, the desert lakes at Yasmina and Dayet Srji and the auberges most popular with birdwatchers such as Yasmina, Derkaoua and Caravane. This is the best area for Desert Sparrow and Spotted Sandgrouse and species such as Desert Warbler, Egyptian Nightjar, Saharan Olivaceous Warbler and Fulvous Babbler are also seen regularly (see page 10).

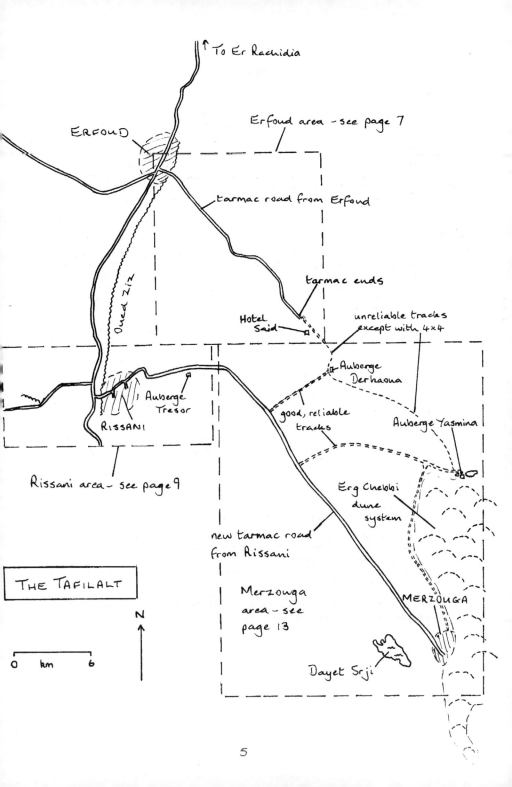

Erfoud

Attraction

The road into the desert from Erfoud takes you to some of the most reliable spots for Desert Warbler and sites where Egyptian Nightjar and Desert Sparrow have been found in some years.

Getting there

The road into the desert is the one that leads from the north-east corner of the main square. You can find the square by taking either of the two main roads that run east from the main road through town (eg at 31°26'7.59"N 4°13'59.82"W), 500 or 600 metres north of where the main road meets the road from Jorf. Leaving the square behind, you'll need to cross the ford of the River Ziz and drive on, keeping the hill fort to your left.

Notes

1. Where the road crosses the Ziz (31.4321 N 4.2267 W), it is possible to walk beside the river which in places is lined with rushes. Both Little and Baillon's Crakes have been seen here in the distant past; the best bird I had in April 2009 was a Moroccan White Wagtail. The drive south from Erfoud used to be a guaranteed spot for up to 50 Brown-necked Raven but they're now much more difficult to see since the eye-sore of a rubbish dump here has been miraculously tidied up. Mourning Wheatear has also been seen here in the past.

2. One of my favourite spots for Desert Warbler is by the road, 6.3 km after the River Ziz, where fossil diggers have left piles of dark stones in a line which crosses the road (31.3900 N 4.1831 W). Search in the patch of land just east of the road with lots of short thorny bushes. In winter there's a chance of Desert Warblers (and Tristram's Warbler too) in any of the little roadside bushes around here but in spring they are more confined to breeding sites such as this one (though I failed to find them here in 2009). Other desert birds to look for in this area include Hoopoe Larks, Bar-tailed Desert Larks, Cream-coloured Coursers and Desert Wheatears. The ridge of cliffs just south of here is said to be a site for Pharaoh Eagle Owl.

3. 9.9 km from Erfoud, the road passes over a ridge between two sets of rocks. Park just beyond here where there's a fossil stall next to a line of roadside tamarisks (31.3690 N 4.1518 W) and walk the bushy wadi in either direction. This is a particularly good spot for wintering warblers; I've had up to a dozen Tristram's Warblers as well as Desert, Dartford and Spectacled Warblers. It's also a regular site for Egyptian Nightjar, especially about 100 metres to the south of the road. I failed to find them here in 2005 but in the same year Tim Farr and others had them 'churring' around a hotel nearby. To get there, drive a further 2.1 km and turn east where a track leads to the new hotel, 1 km from the road. The oasis and cultivated areas around the hotel were also good for migrants including Western Olivaceous and Melodious Warblers.

4. 17 km from Erfoud, the tarmac ends but the pistes are well maintained for a further 2.3 km, as far as the new Hotel Said. This acquired ornithological fame a few years ago when Desert Sparrows were seen here, especially around a rubbish tip at the south-west side of the compound. Like several others I failed to find that species here in 2009 but the hotel has anyway remained popular as maybe the best site for Desert Warbler. In trip reports this is repeatedly described as 'in a sand-dune covered wadi 400 metres south of the kasbah' but in fact the wadi is a full kilometre from the hotel (31.3067 N 4.0990 W). Nigel Redman has confirmed that he's found them there almost every year for 30 years.

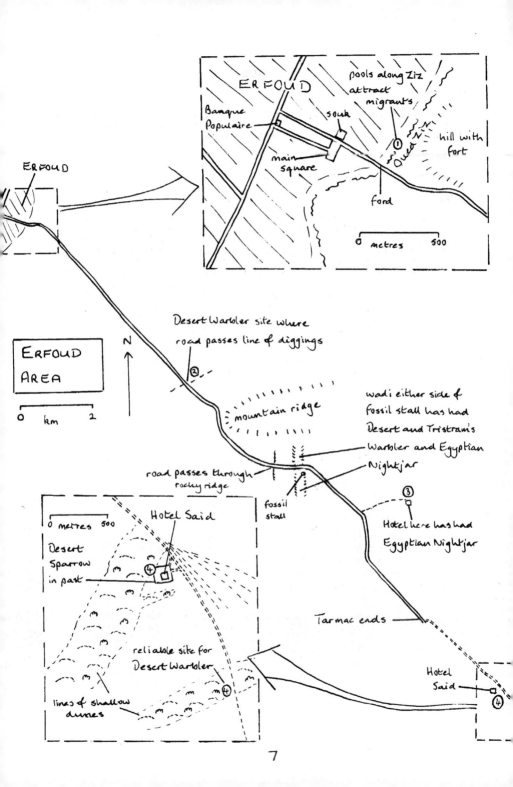

Rissani

Attraction

If you're going to the desert areas around Merzouga, you'll almost certainly have to go through Rissani but it's worth spending some time here as this area has probably the best stake-outs for Saharan Olivaceous Warbler, Pharaoh Eagle owl and Egyptian Nightjar.

Getting there

Easily reached by travelling south through Erfoud and continuing for 18 km.

Notes

1. This is probably the easiest site for finding 'Saharan Olivaceous Warbler' – and being sure of what you've got! There are two species of Olivaceous Warbler breeding in this area: the most widespread is the Western Olivaceous Warbler, likely to be encountered in the gardens, date palms and cultivated areas around both Erfoud and Rissani. This is the same species *Hippolais opaca* as can be found in Spain and the rest of Morocco. However, there is another form *Hippolais pallida reiseri* which also occurs here. It is currently 'lumped' as a race of Eastern Olivaceous Warbler but some would argue that it deserves recognition as a distinct species 'Saharan Olivaceous Warbler'. Visually, it can be difficult to tell the two species apart, but Saharan Olivaceous Warbler lacks the heavy-billed and long, flat-headed appearance of *opaca* and is more likely to show repeated tail-flicking. However, the best way to tell them apart is by their song: Saharan Olivaceous Warbler keeps on repeating the same motifs in a rising and falling cyclical rhythm (eg 'chak-chakara swi-swi SWEE SWEE.. chak chakara swi-swi SWEE SWEE'). The song of Western Olivaceous Warbler lacks both the regular repetition and the marked rising and falling and so is more of a monotonous scratchy chatter. The best-known site for Saharan Olivaceous Warbler is in the tamarisks (they seem to be found almost exclusively in tamarisks) along the banks of the River Ziz either side of the bridge to the west of Rissani (31.2781 N 4.2799 W). It's worth making this one of your first stops in the area in order to learn the distinctive song and try to establish the visual differences too. Walk from the bridge in either direction and you should encounter several singing birds. I found at least 3 males by walking to the bushes 150 metres north of the bridge. I had Blue-cheeked Bee-eater here too.

2. There is a 'circuit touristique' around Rissani which takes you through several small villages and through date palms and small-holdings. Just drive along this route and stop wherever it looks interesting. The commonest species include Western Olivaceous Warbler, Rufous Bush Chat, White-crowned Black wheatear, House Bunting, Hoopoe, Common Bulbul and one of the big-billed races of Crested Lark. Other birds to look out for include Lanner Falcon, Blue-cheeked Bee-eater and Little Owl. Always keep an ear open for the distinctive 'rising whistle' notes of Fulvous Babblers eg in 2009 we had a party of them at 31.2542 N 4.2850 W.

3. In recent years, most crews have visited a site near Rissani for Pharaoh Eagle Owl as described in a trip report by Chris Batty. To get there, take the road out of Rissani, back towards Erfoud but turn left (towards Ouarzazate) at the Ziz petrol station just out of town. Follow this road for 4.8 km and park on the right, just before you meet the rocky ridge on the right. The owls nest on this ridge, just beyond sight of the road, so you'll need to walk for just over 2 km to see them. Follow the wadi beneath the ridge until, after the two areas where sand is piled up against the ridge, you see ahead of you a second much lower ridge (more of a mound), parallel to the main one. Walk up onto this mound and scan the main ridge from there (31.2798 N 4.3566 W). Three perching points for the owls are shown in my DVD 'Finding Birds in Morocco: the deserts'. The first is a hole shaped like a vertical rectangle, the second is on a vertical fissure and is usually marked by white streaks of droppings and the third is in the tumble of rocks much lower down below the main rock face. On my visit in 2009, one bird was at the second site, which looks like it might be where the nest is. The other adult was seen at much closer range at the third spot. I certainly would have missed such terrific views of this bird if it hadn't been pointed out to me by a 'guide' who had tagged along. He called himself 'Ali the Nomad' and I was delighted to reward him with a small payment. You may be able to find the birds without the help of such a guide

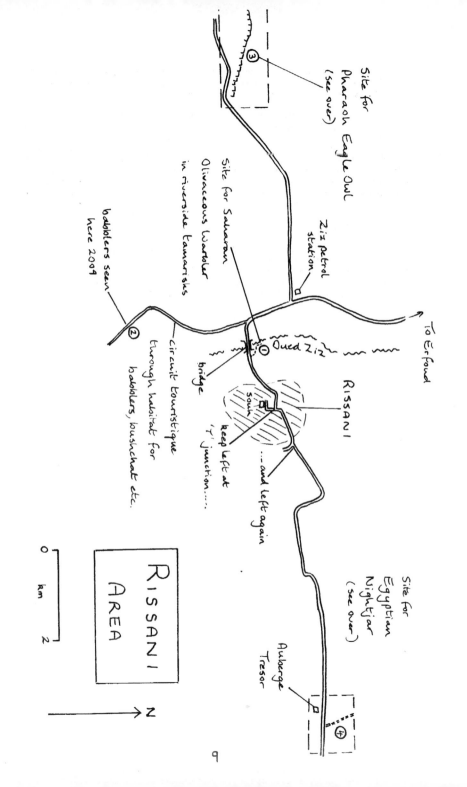

but it can only do good for the locals to discover there's a financial incentive for ensuring the birds don't get disturbed. You are also likely to see Trumpeter Finch and Brown-necked Raven here and Tristram's Warbler has been found in the wadi in winter

4. For many years, the best-known site for Egyptian Nightjar in Morocco has been by the swimming pool at the Auberge Derkaoua (see page 12). However, in recent years there have been rather few sightings there, so this site near Rissani has become the new hotspot. It was the owner of the Auberge Derkaoua who told me in 2005 that he regularly saw them sitting on the the road at night near the Auberge Tresor but I searched unsuccessfully there. However, in the same year, Belgian birder, Michel Watelet, managed to photograph one in daylight in the nearby desert; I published his pictures and accompanying site description in an article at www.birdguides.com (subscribers only). I therefore tried again in 2009 and found at least 3 males singing constantly in calm conditions but hardly at all if it was windy. The Auberge Tresor is about 8 km east of Rissani on the tarmac road to Merzouga (drive through Rissani keeping left at every major junction). Drive 300 metres past the Auberge Tresor and turn left onto a rough track that leads north from the road (31.2941 N 4.1913 W). This track continues for about 800 metres but you may as well park near the road and walk because the nightjars could be found at any point from here. Places where I heard them are shown on the map. However, the best spot was to the east of this track where one of several paths crossed a large bare stony wadi (31.2974 N 4.1897 W). Here I had a bird floating around me at dawn, not only singing but also calling like a Red Grouse (presumably the equivalent of the 'go-ic' call of Eurasian Nightjar) and sitting on the ground within feet of me.

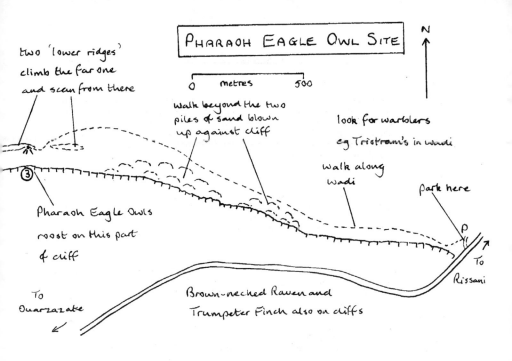

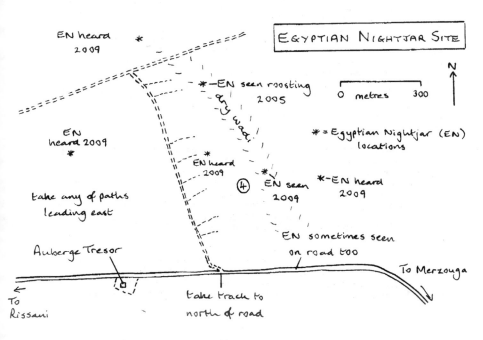

Merzouga

Attraction

You haven't seen the deserts of Morocco until you've been to the areas around Merzouga. This is 'classic' desert complete with sand dunes and camel trains and the best-known place in Morocco for Desert Sparrow and Houbara Bustard. It's also good for Spotted Sandgrouse, Brown-necked Raven, both Olivaceous Warblers, Desert Warbler, Fulvous Babbler and, at least in some years, Egyptian Nightjar. In relatively wet seasons, temporary lakes form here which support breeding waterbirds such as Ruddy Shelduck and many migrants.

Getting there

As you enter Rissani, keep left at every major road junction, following signs to either Merzouga or Taouz. Once out of Rissani, look for metal roadside signs indicating the best piste for each auberge. The turn off for Derkaoua is about 14 km from Rissani, the Yasmina turn off is after about 18.5 km and the turn off to Dayet Srji is to the right at 35.5 km just before you reach Merzouga.

Notes

1. Until recently, the Auberge Kasbah Derkaoua (31.2902 N 4.0919 W) was the place to see Egyptian Nightjar, most famously flying around, or even sitting beside, the swimming pool at night. However, despite being seen in March 09, they have been absent, or at least difficult, here in several recent years. Note that one observer failed to find them at night but then succeeded by getting up before daylight the following morning. The Auberge Tresor (page10) is now a more reliable site for this species. However, the grounds still provide lots of cover for migrants so there's very enjoyable birding to be had here anyway. It used to be the case that birders couldn't visit here unless they were staying at the hotel. Many have considered the prices (550 Dh per person for half board in 2009) to be a bit steep, which it certainly is by Moroccan standards, but really £42 pounds a night isn't too bad for a smart hotel with a 3-course meal included. However, a cheaper alternative is available – groups of up to 8 birders can pay 40dh (about £3) an hour per person to wander around the grounds in search of birds. In addition to regular Western Bonelli's and Western Orphean Warblers in spring and Tristram's Warblers in winter, this is one of the more regular locations for Fulvous Babbler (try around the back of the buildings). Desert Sparrow has been recorded here, though not for some years. Don't be confused by the loud squawks you will hear from their tame parrot. The wadi to the north of the auberge is also worth checking; there you could find Hoopoe Lark, Bar-tailed Desert Lark, Desert Wheatear, White-crowned Black Wheatear, Black-eared Wheatear, Trumpeter Finch, Moussier's Redstart, Southern Grey Shrike, Short-toed Lark and the desert race of Crested Lark. Desert Warbler and Egyptian Nightjar have also been found in the wadi. Although this place is only 3 km from the Kasbah Said, it's now safer to get here the 'long way round' by taking the piste from the Merzouga road and following the pale green markers for 6.5 km (not 5 km as advertised!)

2. Seemingly the days are gone when you could find flocks of up to 80 Desert Sparrows amongst the camel dung behind the Café Yasmina (31.2137 N 3.9887 W) – in most recent years there have been none there at all, though I did have two in 2005. However, the café, which has now grown into an auberge with excellent facilities, is still my favourite place to stay in the desert, right next to the spectacular sand dunes of the Erg Chebbi. Immediately to the east of the auberge is a copse of tamarisks which provides an exciting migrant trap. This has been recognized by the Institute of Catalan Ornithology who maintain a ringing station there throughout the spring, getting to grips (literally) with the birds that pass through. By talking to the ringers you may get news of what's about and possibly views of birds such as Western and Saharan Olivaceous Warblers in the hand (in April 2009 they were catching both these species every day). You can see these birds yourself just by standing still at a spot amongst the tamarisks and watching flycatchers, nightingales, redstarts and warblers coming down to little freshwater pools. In some years there will also be rather large pools here, in fact two lakes, one either side of the auberge. These will attract waterbirds; in 2009 there were several pairs of

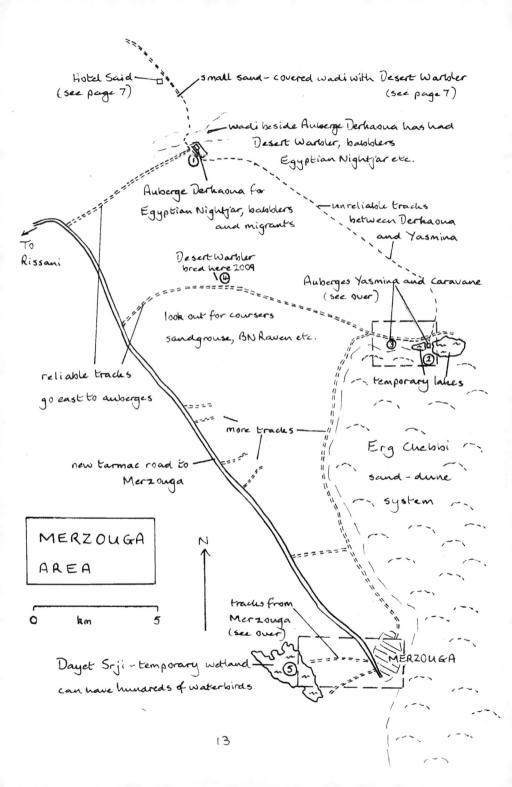

Ruddy Shelduck breeding here and Marbled Duck is sometimes seen. The lake may also attract sandgrouse to drink although 47 Spotted Sandgrouse here on 3rd May 2007 (Fraser Simpson) was exceptional. A White-crowned Black Wheatear roosts in the dining room each night and other species in the area include Bar-tailed Desert Lark, Hoopoe Lark and Brown-necked Raven. There's also a birders' log kept here which can provide invaluable notes on where key species have been seen. To reach Yasmina, follow signs and stone markers from the Rissani road and bump your way across the desert for about 13 kilometres.

3. The new hotspot for Desert Sparrow is the Auberge Caravane (31.2152 N 4.0012 W), literally the next auberge to Yasmina, just over a kilometre to the west. In recent years this has been the only site where birds can be more or less guaranteed – but even here there are only a few of them. Although some can be seen around the auberge itself, an even more reliable spot is the little goat shed (31.2166 N 4.0009 W) by the main piste about 150 metres north of the auberge. Around the walls of this shed are a number of holes in which many House Sparrows will be nesting but for some years at least one of those holes has had a pair of Desert Sparrows too. In 2009 they were in the wall facing the main piste, literally a few feet from it. If you struggle to find them here, don't forget to try the areas where camels are kept – they do have a liking for areas of camel dung.

4. The piste between the Rissani-Merzouga road and the Auberge Yasmina is good for most of the 'true' desert species such as Hoopoe Lark, Bar-tailed Desert Lark, Cream-coloured Courser and Brown-necked Raven. In 2009 I also had a group of 3 Spotted Sandgrouse flying over (usually a tricky species to find) and Roger Sanmarti found a breeding pair of Desert Warblers as indicated on the map (31.2415 N 4.0834 W).

5. If the winter has been wet enough, a temporary lake, the Dayet Srji, may form to the west of Merzouga. At such times there may be lots of waders, ducks, terns and flamingoes; Ruddy Shelducks occur regularly and Morocco's first Kittlitz's Plovers and Pink-backed Pelicans were found here. In the wet spring of 2007, the lake had not only hundreds of Ruddy Shelduck and over 100 flamingoes but also 100+ Marbled Duck, 4 Red-knobbed Coot and a variety of waders that included Marsh Sandpiper and Temminck's Stint. Even when there is no water, the lake basin can be attractive to birds such as numerous warblers around the tamarisks, including Desert and Tristram's, and up to a thousand Trumpeter Finch. Lanner Falcons often hunt around here. To reach the lake you just need to follow one of the tracks leading west from Merzouga as shown on the map (eg from 31.1039 N 4.0201 W).

6. (not illustrated). It is possible to hire a guide to take you further into the desert in a 4x4 vehicle in search of Houbara Bustards. Some of these guides are excellent as they are in cahoots with 'guardians' who are paid to protect nesting pairs of bustards and therefore not only know where to look but also have permission to go there without disturbing the birds. Almost everyone you meet around Merzouga will claim to be a guide and not all of them have the necessary knowledge so it is probably better to negotiate two prices before you set off – one if you do see the birds and another if you don't. One birder's log recommends Ali Mouni from the Hotel Nomad (4 Houbaras seen on a trip in January 08). Incidentally, if you try exploring here without a guide, even if you don't get stuck in sand, you could easily get lost and end up in Algeria (only 18 km from Yasmina) where you may get arrested.

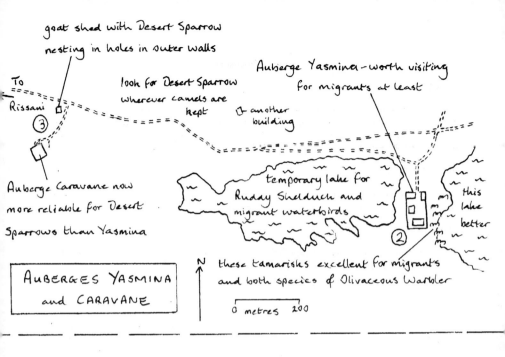
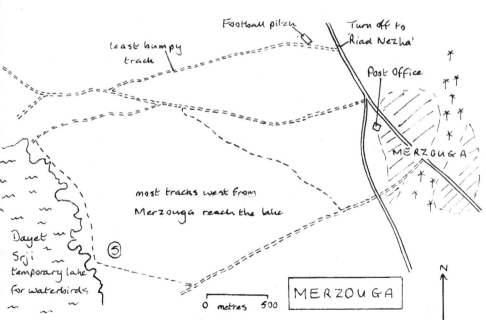

Erfoud to Boumalne

Attraction

Between Erfoud and Boumalne are a number of sites worth checking for certain species. By taking detours from the main route you can check out what is probably the best site in Morocco for Scrub Warbler and visit the magnificent Gorge du Todra which has wintering Tristram's Warbler and breeding Bonelli's Eagles.

Getting there

There is a perfectly good road from Erfoud to Boumalne via Jorf. You can detour by turning east near Tinejdad towards Er Rachidia or north to the Gorge du Todra just east of Tinerhir.

Notes

1. During the drive from Erfoud towards Jorf, look out in the palm groves and cultivated areas for species such as Blue-cheeked Bee-eater, Lanner Falcon, Southern Grey Shrike and Rufous Bush Chat, all of which may be spotted on the many telegraph posts and wires. There are Fulvous Babblers here too.

2. A contributor to one of the birders' logs has commented that 'Jorf is a waste of time and should be scrubbed from all itineraries'. I'm inclined to agree with him since it has taken me several visits to muster Hoopoe Lark, Desert Lark, Cream-coloured Courser and White-crowned Black Wheatear. It's now many years since species such as Fulvous Babbler, Desert Warbler and even the elusive Scrub Warbler have been seen in the deserts around the piles of diggings west of Jorf.

3. In recent years, many birding crews have failed to find Scrub Warbler in Morocco but there is one site which still seems to be reliable. It's generally referred to as km43 from Er Rachidia, though it's actually closer to the next km post. Between km43 and km44 west of Er Rachidia, park where the road crosses a broad but shallow wadi (31.7548 N 4.8330 W). (The road here has been strengthened and marked with red and white painted edgings). Looking north-west from this 'bridge' you'll see a lone dark bush, then other bushes beyond that – it's those far bushes (31.7600 N 4.8528 W) almost 2 km from the road that you need to aim for, following the line of ankle-high vegetation that marks the course of the wadi. In April 09, a pair of Scrub Warblers were obviously breeding here (carrying food for young), as were a pair of Spectacled Warblers. Others have seen Desert Warblers in this wadi too.

4. The Gorge du Todra is worth a visit for the scenery alone but should be avoided at weekends or holidays when hundreds of locals come here to party. Turn off just east of Tinerhir where the river Todra crosses the P32 and continue through villages then oases to the main gorge. The river here is easily fordable and, for a fee, you can park by the restaurants in the gorge. Here you should see Grey Wagtail, Black Redstart, Blue Rock Thrush and lots of Crag Martins. Rumours of African Rock Martins here, and indeed anywhere in the High Atlas mountains, seem to be unsubstantiated (but see page 24). It is said that Bonelli's Eagles nest in the cliffs above the cafes but, although I have seen the adults several times (including 2009), I've never managed to work out where the nest is. Beyond the gorge, the valley gets wider; this area is worth checking for Rock Bunting and Tristram's Warbler (though House Bunting and Dartford Warbler also occur) but most visitors fail to see the Lammergeier that is also reputed to be here.

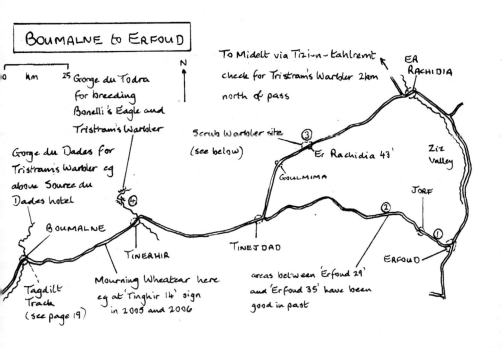

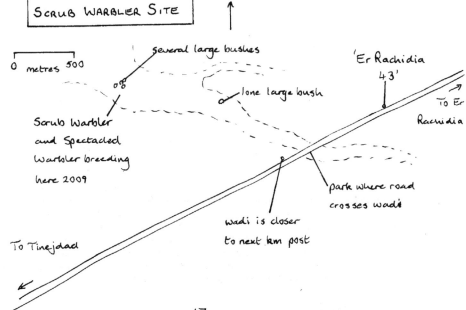

Boumalne du Dades and the Tagdilt Track

Attraction

The best-known area in Morocco for desert-loving larks and wheatears, almost all of which can be found here. Some species such as Red-rumped Wheatear, Temminck's Horned Lark and Thick-billed Lark are usually more numerous here than at any other known site and more birders see Crowned Sandgrouse here than anywhere else in Morocco. Houbara Bustard and Pharaoh Eagle Owl are also possible.

Getting there

Boumalne is on the main P32 road between Ouarzazate (124 km) and Er Rachidia (185 km). The track(s) to Tagdilt lead south from this road at various points east of Boumalne.

Notes

1. For recent news of birds in this area there's an excellent birders' log-book in the Auberge Soleil Bleu (31.3779 N 5.9814 W). This cheap, basic but very friendly establishment serves wonderful Moroccan food and is justifiably very popular with visiting birdwatchers. (Beware though, it can be very cold in winter). The yard and the breakfast verandah can be excellent for watching House Buntings, Desert Larks and Black Wheatears.

2. To find the 'original' Tagdilt track' you should turn south from the main road, either down the east side of the barracks, or (better) just west of the 'Tinghir 48' km post (31.3665 N 5.9613 W). The various larks and wheatears are generally widespread around here, but a popular area is west of the track around the 'first wadi'. Houbaras have been seen on this plain several times and Eagle Owls have been seen even in the small rocky gullies formed by the shallow wadis. Red-rumped Wheatear is usually the commonest passerine and you shouldn't have to walk far before finding Temminck's Horned Lark. Sandgrouse tend to fly over such a large area that they could be seen from anywhere, although the Ikniouen road (site 5) may be a better bet. Of the other species, Desert and Bar-tailed Desert Lark are both possible, though irregular, and, in winter, Thick-billed and Lesser Short-toed Larks may occur in flocks of several hundred. Both these species usually decline in the spring; they may remain tolerably common or both be virtually absent. From early March, the declining Lesser Short-toed Larks become replaced by hundreds of migrating Short-toed Larks. Long-legged Buzzards and Lanner Falcons are usually seen eventually, the buzzards often reaching double figures in winter. Common Ravens are often present amongst the refuse closer to town; some observers insist that they've also seen Brown-necked Raven here. There have also been 2 sightings of Crimson-winged Finch around the refuse, although Trumpeter Finches are much more likely, especially by the wadis. Other desert species may occur here but you are more likely to find them at Site 3.

3. Beyond what I call the 'main wadi', the land rises to create a slightly higher plateau, rather sandier with less vegetation. This is a much better area for Hoopoe Lark; a careful search should produce a count in double figures. Late February onwards sees the arrival of up to 50 Cream-coloured Coursers and lots of Desert Wheatears which almost replace the Red-rumped Wheatears as the commonest bird on this sandier ground. Thick-billed Larks are often more numerous here and you should see Thekla Larks too. Other species reported have included Northern Wheatear (regular), Skylark (absent most years), Isabelline Wheatear (once), Stone Curlew, Tawny Pipit and Shorelark (very rare).

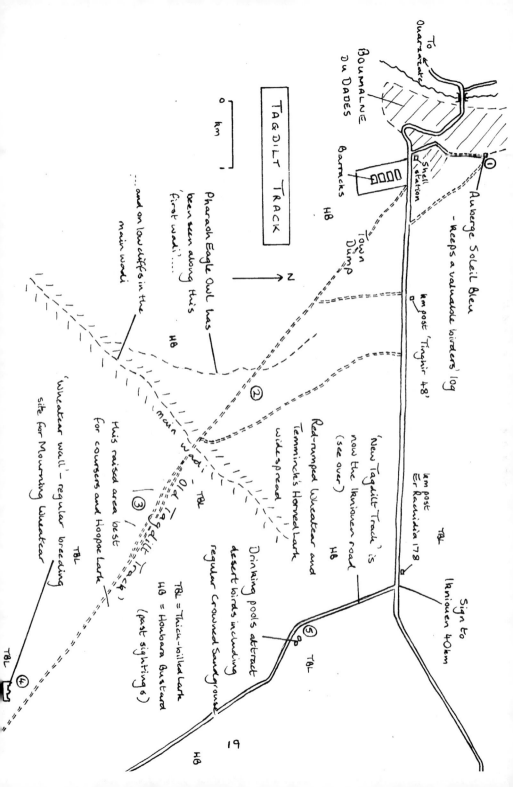

4. By driving beyond the main wadi for a further 4.5 km you will see a ruined building on your right (31.3104 N 5.9007 W). This is what I call 'wheatear wall'. In 2005 3 species of wheatear seemed to be breeding here: Desert, White-crowned and Mourning Wheatear. The Mourning Wheatears were seen here again in 2007 and 2008 and were still there on my visit in 2009. At last – a regular site for Mourning Wheatear. Beyond here are cultivated areas that can act as migrant traps. Look here for Melodious Warbler, Wryneck, Bonelli's Warbler, etc. as well as Tree Pipits, Garden Warblers, Redstarts, etc.

5. What was previously described as the 'new Tagdilt track' has now become a tarmac road giving much easier access to this whole area. It is found by driving 6 km east from Boumalne then looking for sign to 'Ikniouen 40'. Perhaps the main claim to fame for this new road is the fact that it passes a spot which, at least during 2008 and 2009 regularly had standing water and was therefore a magnet for birds coming to drink, including larks, wheatears, wagtails, Trumpeter Finch and, most significantly, sandgrouse. They are not guaranteed but many observers have reported seeing up to 22 Crowned Sandgrouse here; Black-bellied and Pin-tailed Sandgrouse are also possible. To find this site (31.3503 N 5.9068 W), drive 1.8 km down the Ikniouen road and look in the hollow areas immediately to the left (just after a left-hand bend). The water is in depressions so may not be visible from the road; you may have to wander 100 metres or so to find the pools. The sandgrouse are most likely to appear between 8.00 and 10.00hrs. The surrounding areas support the usual Tagdilt track species, including, in 2009, a few Thick-billed Larks, though you still need to reach site 3 for the best chance of Hoopoe Lark and Courser. This is one of several spots where Houbaras have been seen in the past so scan carefully early in the morning for a 'waving white flag'. Sightings in the Tagdilt area were reported in the log for 2005 (4-5 birds!), 2006 and 2008 but I failed to find one in 2009 despite two dawn starts and determined scanning.

6. After 6.5 km (from the main road) look for a track to the west towards a rather incongruous arch in the middle of the desert. This track presumably gives much easier access to the wheatear wall (site 4) which is now only 2 km from the road. This area, around where the Tagdilt track meets the Ikniouen road, has previously been good for all three species of sandgrouse (worth trying if the pools at site 5 are dry) and Thick-billed Lark. I've had displaying Houbara here and Dupont's Lark has been found twice.

7. 10.5 km from the main road you'll find a copse of trees to your left with a small freshwater reservoir (31.2919 N 5.8542 W). What a fantastic migrant trap this should be; I had Western Bonelli's Warbler and Pied Flycatcher on my brief visit in 2009.

Ikniouen Road

main road Boumalne – Tinerhir

sign to 'Ikniouen 40'

⑤ — sand grouse, especially Crowned, likely to visit these drinking pools unless dry

pools also attract larks, wheatears and wagtails etc.

N ↑

0 — km — 1

good area for coursers, Hoopoe Lark, TB Lark etc

'Old Tagdilt Track'

'Wheatear wall'

access to 'Wheatear wall' from here

⑥

cultivated areas can be good for migrants

This area has had Houbara, Dupont's and 3 species of sandgrouse

pond and orchard for migrants

Sign to 'Tagdilt'

low dark hills likely to have Pharaoh Eagle Owl

⑦

Ikniouen

Tagdilt ↓

Around Ouarzazate

Attraction

The roads either side of Ouarzazate, between Boumalne and Taliouine, offer ample opportunities to see birds such as Desert Lark, Black Wheatear, Thekla Lark and Trumpeter Finch. They also pass through areas of high-altitude plains that can be great for Thick-billed Larks, Cream-coloured Coursers and Black-bellied and Pin-tailed Sandgrouse. However, they are perhaps best known as being, until recently, the most likely places to see Mourning Wheatear in Morocco (see also page 20 site 4).

Getting there

See map opposite

Notes

1. Moroccan White Wagtail (*Motacilla alba subpersonata*) is generally rather scarce at most of the known birding sites so if you fail elsewhere, it may be worth checking along the shores of the river that runs parallel to the road, on the northern side, just west of El Kelaa. In my experience this race is always associated with freshwater habitats.

2. Until recently, most reports of Mourning Wheatear were of birds 'fluked' beside the roads either side of Ouarzazate. To the east of Ouarzazate, birds have been reported at 'El Kelaa 45', 'El Kelaa 34' (which may be the same site as 'Ouarzazate 46'), and 'El Kelaa 27' (which may be the same as 'Ouarzazate 55' where Chris Batty had a pair nesting in 2004). To the west of Ouarzazate, Richard Bonser had a pair beside 'Ouarzazate 29' in 2005.

3. The Barrage El Mansour, a reservoir just east of Ouarzazate, can be good for waterbirds, including ducks, waders, gulls, terns and herons. Ruddy Shelduck breeds here and hundreds have been counted in winter. Marbled Duck can be numerous and 4 species of sandgrouse have also been recorded. The reservoir can be reached from several roads leading south from the P32 as you drive east from Ouarzazate. Alternatively before you leave the east end of town, take the right turn at the traffic lights signposted to Ait Kdif (see map at www.findingbirds.com).

4. The minor road to the south of Amerzgane has become popular as a likely spot for both Mourning Wheatear and Thick-billed Lark. Other species seen here include Desert Lark and Trumpeter Finch. This road can be found by turning south in Amerzgane (31.0443N 7.2109W) or north from 30.9548"N 7.2058W.

5. The plain 5 km west of Taznakt has previously been good for Trumpeter Finch and flocks of Thick-billed Lark (a highly nomadic species that can be numerous one year but absent the next).

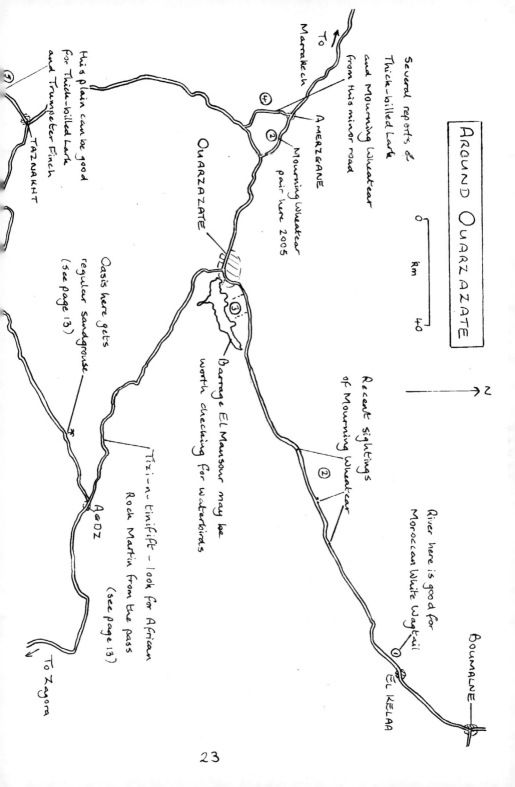

The Jbel Bani route - Goulimine to Mhamid

Attraction

The routes along the northern edge of the Jbel Bani mountain range have now been opened to tourists, giving birders a new part of Morocco to explore. This area will surely have more sites for species such as Desert Sparrow, Egyptian Nightjar, Spotted Sandgrouse, Scrub Warbler and Fulvous Babbler just waiting to be discovered; Lichtenstein's Sandgrouse is more likely here than anywhere else. Here's a chance to break new ground.

Getting there

The solid lines on the map indicate reasonable roads that can be reached in an ordinary car. The dotted lines indicate routes that are best taken in a 4x4 vehicle.

Notes

1. The Scrub Warblers in this part of Morocco are of the much darker race *theresae*. However, as some observers have failed to find them at the best-known site (page 30, site 1), maybe it's worth repeating that in 1994 I had 3 Scrub Warblers at a site about 70 km east of Bou Izakarn, just a few km short of the turning to Tagoujgalte. To the south of the road is a low hill, beyond which is a plain and wadi which eventually yielded 30 Desert Lark, 2 Bar-tailed Desert Lark, 6 Theklas, Desert Wheatear, Spectacled Warbler, Tristram's Warbler and 9 Fulvous Babblers, as well as the Scrub Warblers. The wadi crosses the road at 29.1079 N 9.1534 W - you can park and walk south-east from there. Also, 6 Black-bellied Sandgrouse flew over and 2 distant Golden Eagles were over the mountains to the south.

2. Bergier and Bergier (2003) suggest that Tata would be a good place to stop and explore, with Fulvous Babblers in wadis to the east of town and a palm grove 18 km to the south of town (just east of the road, presumably at 29.6193 N 7.9997 W) where they had dozens of Spotted Sandgrouse coming to drink.

3. Apparently a better place for sandgrouse is at Tissint where a cliff at the north-east edge of town overlooks pools that have attracted Black-bellied, Crowned and Spotted Sandgrouse. Bergier and Bergier (2003) also report a nearby site for Lichtenstein's Sandgrouse; a flock came to drink by the Oued Tissint, 10 km south-east of the town one evening in January 2002.

4. Another site for sandgrouse is 12 km west of Agdz, where a roadside palm grove overlooks the Oued Tamsift. The western end of the palms is best (park at 30.6529 N 6.5659 W). In 2005 there were only limited pools here so it was easy to get close views of birds such as Trumpeter Finch, Desert Lark and Rufous Bush Chat coming to drink. Black-bellied Sandgrouse flew around but did not settle and Blue-cheeked Bee-eaters seemed to be breeding. In 2009 when there was water all along the wadi, the same birds were harder to see well and I didn't see any sandgrouse.

5. About 16 km west of Agdz, the pass at Tizi-n-Tinifift is a well-known site for African Rock Martin. They can be seen by looking into the gorge from the car park at 30.7103 N 6.5893 W. The same site is also good for Black Wheatear and Desert Lark

6. The areas around Mhamid, on the Algerian border, south of Zagora, are good for desert species including Fulvous Babbler, Lanner Falcon and Desert Sparrow. There's a Bedouin camp in the dunes west of M'hamid which can only be reached with a 4x4 vehicle but one bird tour group had 15 Desert Sparrows there in 2009.

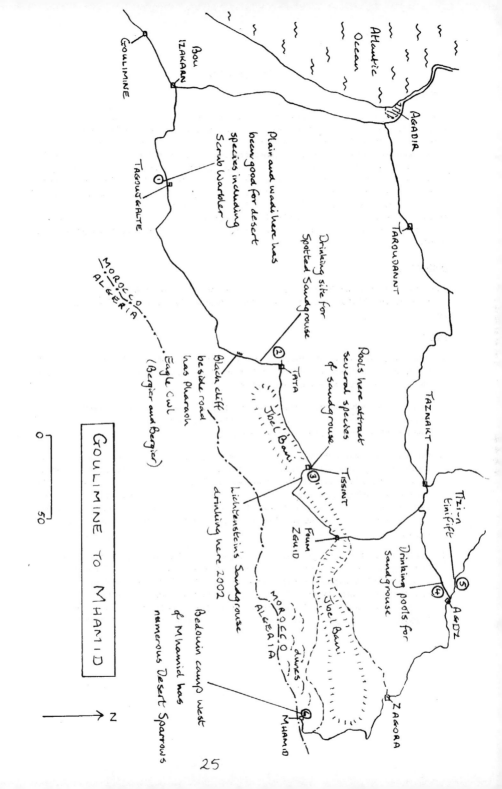

The Sous Valley

Attraction

This the only place in the world where the Argan tree grows, producing a savannah-type habitat much loved by birds of prey. In 1993 I visited this area with W.H. Payn who recalled his previous trip here in 1938 with Col. Meinerzhagen when they had Double-spurred Francolin, as well as perhaps a dozen sightings of Chanting Goshawks. Those days are long gone. In the 1990's there was still a chance of seeing Chanting Goshawks and Tawny Eagles but now those species seem to have gone completely perhaps because the Argan scrub is now much depleted due to the development of vast olive and orange groves and over-grazing by tree-climbing goats. Even so, this area still has good birds including Fulvous Babbler, Little Swift, Black-shouldered Kite, Barbary Falcon. 'Moroccan' Magpie, Western Orphean Warbler and Red-necked Nightjar. Even better, there is now a known site here where desert species such as Hoopoe Lark, Desert Wheatear and even Egyptian Nightjar can be found.

Getting there

These sites are accessible from the P32 which passes along the Sous valley between Agadir and Taliouine. There is also a new road between Tarouddant and Taliouine which offers new vantage points.

Notes

1. Where the road crosses the river-bed just south-west of Taroudannt, it is possible to walk upstream and, with luck, find Fulvous Babblers and Black-shouldered Kites. At dusk this area is also a well-known site for Red-necked Nightjar.

2. Taroudannt itself has the usual House Buntings, etc. plus a few colonies of Little Swift. These can be seen from many spots; the inexpensive Hotel Saadiens has a rooftop terrace that gives great views over the town so the swifts are easy to pick up.

3. One area of the Sous valley that still has most of the species of the Argan steppe is just behind the delightful l'Arganier d'Or hotel, 19 km east of Tarouddant (30.5532 N 8.6911 W). It is clearly signposted from the main road behind a little village (Ait Igasse). Follow the track down the right hand side of the hotel grounds and within 500 metres you're in good habitat where I've recently seen Fulvous Babbler, Moroccan Magpie, Western Orphean Warbler, Southern Grey Shrike, Rufous Bush Chat etc. I'd be surprised if an evening visit here didn't produce Red-necked Nightjar.

4. Possibly the best area of Argan steppe in the valley is around the village of Tafingoulte, reached by taking the road towards the Tizi-n-Test pass but turning right after 8 km. Continue to good Argan habitat just beyond the village where species such as Thekla Lark, Southern Grey Shrike and Western Orphean Warbler should be easy to find. The area around the football pitch (approx 30.7612 N 8.3892 W) is a well-known site for Red-necked Nightjar – I filmed them there in 2005.

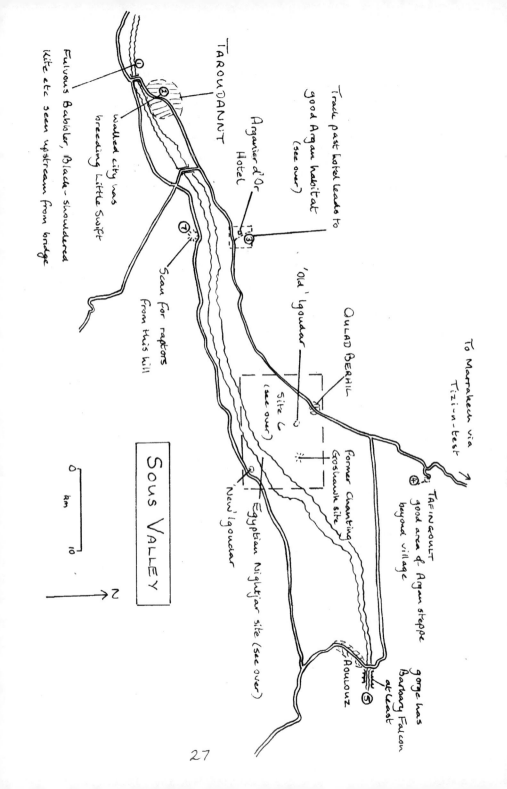

5. The gorge at Aoulouz is no longer a breeding site for Bald Ibis but is still a good spot to look for Barbary Falcon and Long-legged Buzzard. I've previously visited a Lanner Falcon nest site further upstream but have no recent evidence that this species still breeds there.

6. It has recently become known that the river bed of the Oued Sous is a regular site for several breeding pairs of Egyptian Nightjar. Several observers have approached this site from the south but instructions have been confusing because many of the km posts here have their writing obliterated. The best point of access is next to the post which is numbered '56'; it has no other text on it but it would be 'Taliouine 52' and 'Arazane 24' (so if you see other km markers with those names you can gauge how far away you are). If more markings disappear, the best landmark is an obvious village to the north of the road, complete with minaret. According to Google Earth, this village is called Igoudar. This is confusing because there's another village 6.5 km from here on the other side of the river which birders have been calling 'Igoudar' since it was discovered, in the 1990's, that Dark Chanting Goshawk could be seen near there. Surely there can't be two villages of the same name so close together. I don't know which is correct, so I've called them 'New Igoudar' and 'Old Igoudar'. To get to the nightjars from New Igoudar, follow the main road east from the village for 800 metres and turn left at a track by a hut. Follow this track for 600 metres to another hut close to the edge of the wadi and walk from there at dawn or dusk. Some birders have also reached this area via 'Old Igoudar' (which might save a huge detour but involves negotiating much rougher tracks); about 2 km south-west of Oulad Berhil, turn south east at a crossroads, signposted to 'Tleta Igoudar 5'. After 5 km, after passing through 'Old Igoudar', you cross a small riverbed. If you keep left here, along a track past a water pump, you'll come to the hill from which Chanting Goshawks were seen in the 1990's (though apparently there have been no sightings here, or anywhere in the Sous valley this century). Alternatively, if you keep straight on at the little wadi, following a track that passes an orange grove on the right, you can reach the Oued Sous after 4.5 km. At this point, the riverbed of the Oued Sous is 1.8 km wide and, of course, many kilometers long making a stony desert of considerable size. No wonder then that it provides suitable habitat, not just for the Egyptian Nightjars but also for species such as Hoopoe Lark and Desert Wheatear. In 2009 I had these species by walking along the wadi north of New Igoudar. On a windy night, I failed to hear the nightjars at dusk but heard at least two birds rather distantly before sunrise the next morning.

7. If you still fancy looking for raptors in the Sous valley perhaps hoping to prove that Chanting Goshawk or Tawny Eagle are still there, you should pick one of several small hills in the valley. The one near 'Old Igoudar' (see site 7) is one such site but another good spot is shown on the map and there's another 18 km west of Taroudannt, just north of the old road to Agadir. I've seen Black-shouldered Kite, Hen Harrier, Lanner, Barbary Falcon, Long-legged Buzzard, Merlin and (Northern!) Goshawk from these viewpoints.

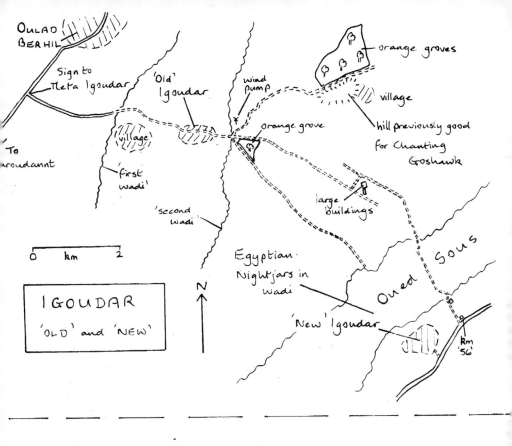
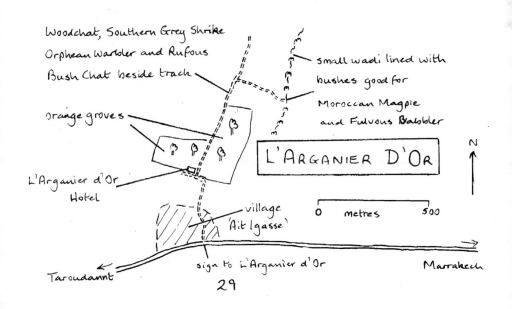

Goulimime
(pronounced Gooly-meem)

Attraction

An opportunity for Agadir-based birdwatchers to see desert birds without travelling East of Ouarzazate. This area has previously received less attention than the famous 'Tagdilt track' near Boumalne but, at least in some winters, it has been better than that site. Apart from an almost comprehensive collection of larks and wheatears, there are also Tawny Eagles, Scrub Warblers and Fulvous Babblers, all more reliable than elsewhere in Morocco. In winter, Lanner Falcon seem to collect here in numbers.

Getting there

Goulimime (Guelmim) is about 200 km from Agadir but you must travel a further 30-40 km towards Tan-Tan to see the best-known desert areas. The main P41 road is generally very good except over the Anti-Atlas mountains, south of Tiznit, where slow trucks could delay you.

Notes

1. Between 7 and 8 km south of Goulimime the road passes over the Oued Sayed. South of the river, the low flat bushes on the right-hand side of the road (28.95767 N 10.1156 W) are a well-known site for Scrub Warbler, a difficult bird elsewhere in Morocco. Up to 20 have been counted here, and I've had up to 4 birds myself, as well as Spectacled Warblers, Red-rumped Wheatear and Desert Wheatear. On the opposite side of the road I've had more Spectacled Warblers, Desert Wheatear, Thekla Larks and Fulvous Babblers. In recent years this site has been much less productive and several birders have complained at seeing little here. However, Scrub Warblers were seen here in 2006 and 2009 at least and other species such as the wheatears and babblers continue to be found by some.

2. Richard Bonser reports that another, possibly more reliable, site for Scrub Warbler is about 5 km further from Goulimime, where the Oued Bauhila passes under the road. In April 2009, he explored along the wadi a few hundred metres east of the bridge and found a family party of about 5 birds (28.9186 N, 10.1433 W). He also had Spectacled Warbler and Rufous Bush Chat. He adds that the Scrub Warblers were found here in 2007 too.

3. It must be possible to find desert birds at any point southwards along the main road. Back in 1993, I stopped at the 'Guelmim 22' kilometre post and quickly had 2 Bar-tailed Desert Larks to the East of the road and 2 Thick-billed Lark, a Trumpeter Finch and Thekla, Short-toed and Lesser Short-toed Larks on the other side. Richard Bonser tells me this site was still good for Thick-billed larks in both 2005 and 2009.

4. After 35 km (from Goulimime) the road passes across a wide sandy plain which the locals are struggling to cultivate. I have previously found the most productive area to be next to the km post 'Tan Tan 100'. By walking north from here for one or two kilometres I've had Hoopoe Lark, Bar-tailed Desert Lark, Desert Lark, Temminck's Horned Lark, both Short-toed Larks, Desert Wheatear, Red-rumped Wheatear, Trumpeter Finch and Cream-coloured Courser. The scattered bushes are well worth checking for warblers; Spectacled, Tristram's, Desert and Scrub Warblers have all been seen. From 09.00 onwards, keep an ear open for sandgrouse; apart from the reliable Black-bellied, I've had up to 30 Crowned Sandgrouse and Spotted Sandgrouse have also been reported (T Davies). Thick-billed Larks are possible here even in years when they are very scarce elsewhere in Morocco. This is reputed to be a very good place for raptors, with up to 20 Lanner Falcons and several Tawny Eagles seen in a day, but I've only had a couple of Lanners and the occasional Long-legged Buzzard. Golden Eagles are also possible (T Davies). In the last 10 years trip reports have suggested that this area is now less

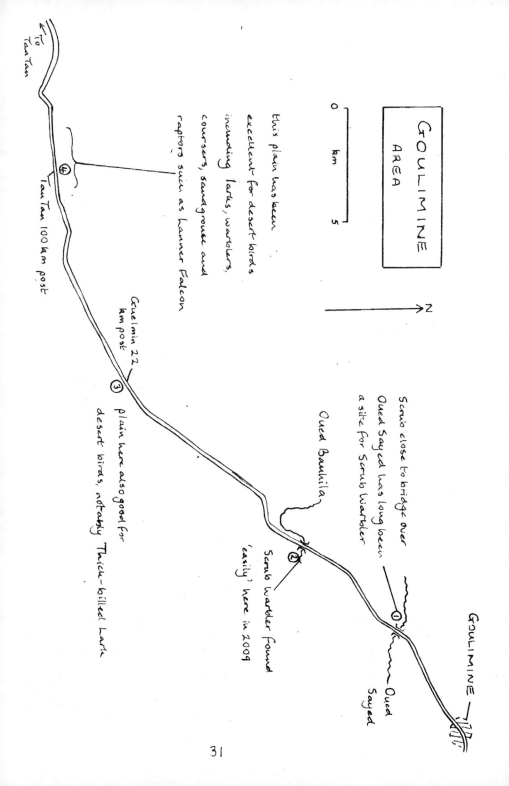

productive although species such as Black-bellied Sandgrouse, Desert Warbler and Thick-billed Lark continue to be seen by some. Some birders have had lots of desert birds elsewhere on the same plain (eg Shaun Robson had '14 Cream-coloured Coursers, 6 Hoopoe Lark, Lanner Falcon, 2 Black-bellied Sandgrouse, c50 Greater Short-toed Larks and up to 1000 Lesser Short-toed Larks' near the Tan Tan 94 post in Nov '94).

Beyond Tan Tan

The areas beyond TanTan have recently become more popular with travelling birders but I'm afraid I haven't managed to visit these areas myself and therefore don't feel able to give them the same treatment as other areas in this book. The main attraction is the fact that the Khnifiss Lagoon, about 240 km beyond the last site in this book, is now a breeding site for several pairs of Cape Gull (*Larus dominicanus vetula*), the African race of Kelp Gull. To see these birds, drive 114km south of Tan Tan Plage and look for a track to the north at 28.0043 N 12.2417 W. Follow this for 2.7 km to the warden's house (28.0283 N 12.2397 W) close to the south shore of the lagoon. By 2009, a few pairs were breeding at the north-east end of the island that can be seen about 1 km from the shore.

En route to here Sue Bryan found Scrub Warbler at a site close to the road 29 km south of Tan Tan in May 2009.

For those who want to be even more adventurous, it is possible to drive as far as Dakhla. The deserts en route to here have several special birds including Desert Sparrow, Black-crowned Finch Lark and, most exciting of all, Cricket Warbler. A site for this species has become known, almost 200 km inland from Dakhla, 41 km before Aoussard, just within the Western Palearctic.